VENICE

Text by Pierre Leprohon
Translated by G. P. Ivins

Minerva
Distributed by Crown Publishers, Inc.

Credits : Archivio B/Ricciarini : 38 - Buga : 8-74 - Blau/Len Sirman : 4 - Dall'Omo/Gemini : end-papers - 6 - 11b - 14 - 16 - 16b - 17a, b - 20a - 24 - 25 - 26a - 27a, b, c - 31a, d - 33 - 34 - 36a - 37b - 39b - 40a, b - 43a - 48a, b - 54b - 55a - 69 - 71 - 75c, d - 77 - 78 - 79 - 80 - 81a - 82 - 83a, b - 85b - 87 - 88 - 94a - Garbison/Fotogram : 21 - 53b - Giraudon : 68 - 93 - Lauros/ Giraudon : 7 - 31b, c - 70 - 92 - Len Sirman : 22 - 47 - 61 - Leprohon : 1 - 2 - 3 - 10 - 11a - 12 - 13 - 18 - 19 - 20b - 28 - 32b - 36b - 39a - 42 - 49 - 50 - 51a, b - 52a, b - 53a - 54a - 55b - 56a, b - 57a, b - 59a, b - 64 - 66 - 67a, b - 73b - 76 - 84 - 85a - 86 - 90a, b, c - 94b - 96 - Mounicq/Fotogram : 63 - Pastor : 16a - 29a, b - 32a - 37a - 43b - 46 - 57c - 58 - 62a, b - 95 - Picou/ Fotogram : 44 - Prenzel/Len Sirman : 60 - Richer/Fotogram : 30 - Roger-Viollet : 5 - Starkey/Camera Press : 72 - Tomsich/ Ricciarini : 9 - 71.

VENICE

Venice—there is not another city like it in the whole world. It is perhaps the most beautiful one, if one judges by its enchanting appearance, the surprise it gives to one's imagination, the spell it casts over one's soul. A city where the power of nature is felt only through its most insubstantial elements, sky and water. The earth beneath it is hardly visible to the eye. Palaces are reflected in the quivering waters. Bridges are seen upside down. Boats float on their own images. Everything is reflection and transparency. It is a city made to delight the eyes and amaze the mind, a city where the dust of centuries dances in the golden mist which bathes the lacelike architecture of the buildings. It is a décor straight out of the "Thousand and One Nights" awaking to the morning light.

Venice has borrowed ideas from far and wide, mixing styles and periods to perfect its enchantments. Like no other city, varying within itself from Gothic grandeur to Baroque exuberance, Venice brings to the borders of Western Europe "the atmosphere of an Eastern tale", to quote the words of Elie Faure. Growing up under the influence of Byzantine architecture, it broke away to adopt the Gothic style.

It has known indignity and pleasure, triumph

In the Piazza San Marco: the lion of Venice and the campanile, two symbols of the city.

3

and decline, pride and humiliation. Its history is that of a state whose conquests were bloody only when its empire was dismembered. When the time of tribulation came it closed up upon its treasures like a jewel-case. It is miraculously intact but fragile and threatened. Treasures? They are deep within its basilicas and on the walls of its museums. They are in the façades of its palaces, along its canals, in the colors of its seasons.

For Venice is not just a city. It is a setting which changes with the light, an atmosphere of fine shades of color transformed by the smallest ray of sunshine. "After rain is the time to see Venice" said Whistler. The cleanwashed sky makes the domes and campaniles of the city stand out. But when the mist billows out, they take on a dreamlike quality.

On sunny days Venice is luminous and tender. On winter evenings Venice glistens moistly under the rainshowers, the streets are no more than wet reflections, and water is everywhere, enveloping everything in a mantle of sadness.

Venice is not a triumphant city. Its past has been too dazzling for its present not to feel the weight of regret for bygone days. But that is why, no doubt, the emotional atmosphere is so subtle and so pervasive.

The picture by the great Venetian painter, Guardi, reproduced opposite, shows the Doges' famous galley, the "Bucentoro", at the traditional ceremony of the "blessing of the sea". Below: a Gothic portal in an alley in Venice.

The Wedding of the Sea

About the year 1000 the Doge Orseolo returned with his victorious fleet from an expedition to put down the Slav pirates who used to ravage the coast of Dalmatia. He was given a hero's welcome, and in gratitude it was decided to mark each Ascension Day with the blessing of the sea. The Bishop of Olivolo, followed by the clergy of Venice, came in procession to the shore to bless the Adriatic which had borne the warships to

victory.

150 years later Pope Alexander III recognised Venice's sovereignty over the Adriatic and sent the Doge a blessed ring which was to be the symbol of Venice's domination of the sea: "Wed the sea every year so that ages yet to come may know that the sea is yours and belongs to you as a wife does to her husband."

From that time dates the tradition of the "wedding of the sea" —*sposalizio del mare*— which replaced the blessing. The Doge's

galley, the "Bucintoro", magnificently carved and gilded, used to take the Doge and his courtiers out to the Lido and thence through the water-gate into the Adriatic. When the galley began to feel the impact of the waves, the Doge threw his golden ring into the sea, saying, "We wed you, o sea, in sign of our true and everlasting dominion." And with its banners streaming in the wind, to loud acclamations and joyous fanfares, the fleet of vessels made its way back through the Grand Canal to St. Mark's.

The sea which had given refuge to the Venetii now assured their triumph. The city of the Doges was now on its way to the peak of its power. But though Venice married the sea, it was also the sea's daughter. Like Venus it was born from the waves. It owed its existence and its prosperity to the sea. The sea was Venice's rampart and for centuries was the source of its fortune and its glory. The city owed everything to the sea and recognised its kinship with her. Venice was and remains the City of the Waters.

1. "THE FINEST STREET IN THE WORLD"

If he arrives in Venice by plane, the traveler will see right away the vast size of the lagoon. Between the shore and the chain of *lidi*, islands are spread out over the blue-green field of this enormous lake. In its center lies Venice, shaped like a swordfish and seeming to attack the mainland.

Whether the traveller approaches by road or rail he will in any case enter the lagoon by the double bridge known as the "Ponte della Liberta". A waterlandscape. Buoys and telegraph posts dot the flat mirror which the passing hours turn into an upside-down sky. A thin horizon line, soon broken by the outline of campaniles. On arrival, the station or garage—*Ferrovia* or *Piazzale Roma*—gives the traveler the privilege of becoming once more a pedestrian for the remainder of his stay.

He will be a dazzled pedestrian, with many surprises in store for him. On leaving the station, whose sober modernism is only a quarter of a century old, Venice, with its animation, its canals, its *vaporetti*, its bridges, churches and palaces, has one in its thrall. Immediately, just as a perfume invades one's senses, one's eyes discover a city quite unlike any other. The best thing is to allow oneself to be carried away, to take, not one of those over-speedy "taxis" also called *motoscafi*, but the *vaporetto* which has just come

Left: aerial view of the Grand Canal. Below: a Renaissance view.

alongside the landing-stage near the sign *Ferrovia*. And to embark for San Marco as if embarking for the underworld.

The palaces of the Grand Canal

Here, at the railway station of Santa Lucia, starts the *Canal Grande,* justly described as "the finest street in the world": a street lined with palaces at whose entrances the uneasy water laps, where boats meet and pass. It is intersected by *rii,* little canals out of which shoots silently the long shape of a black gondola. Here you can see palaces and churches in which all the architectural styles from the thirteenth to eighteenth centuries mingle and overlap. Fantasy and severity, the ostentation of the East and the exuberance of the Baroque, are intermingled. It is a triumphal way whose magic one must open one's heart to, before returning to analyse its charm and examine its riches more closely.

The Grand Canal is the bed of a river, or, to be more exact, a channel which passed through the islands in the center of the lagoon. It has retained its original breadth and its grandeur, and still has the elegant, curving shape which cuts the city in two. It will continue, growing wider and wider, until it comes to an end in front of the Palace of the Doges, where it re-enters the lagoon.

The first impression is one of wonderment,

of astonishment at seeing so much everyday bustle in so ancient a setting. The *vaporetto* crosses from one shore to the other, ferrying groups of passengers who disembark to go about their business. Speeding *motoscafi* churn the canal with their wakes, and there are heavy barges loaded with goods and materials. We will follow the various stages of this "luminous way", where the lapping waves of the present shatter the reflections of the past.

There is a wide quay in front of the station. Opposite it stands the church of San Simeone Piccolo, a reconstruction dating from the 18th century whose massive dome dominates a neo-classical façade. It is a typical example of Venice's last architectural style, to be seen in many variations of the period, blending more or less happily relics of Byzantine art with those of Antiquity. On the same quay, the church of the Scalzi (or Discalced Carmelites) was completed at the end of the 17th century in a Baroque style showing more Roman than Venetian influence.

Thus, right at the beginning of his visit to the Grand Canal, the visitor has an insight into Venice's ecclesiastical architecture, composed of reconstructions, modifications, borrowings and reminiscences, an ostentatious love of show which is in fact the expression of a people and a period demonstrating their faith by the magnificence of their wealth.

Venice has hundreds of churches, many of

Left: the station and the "Ferrovia" vaporetto stop. Opposite: the church of the Scalzi. Below: a balcony of the Palazzetto Falier, a building typical of those along the Grand Canal.

them ancient. But because of fires and rebuilding, little often remains of the original structures but fragments hidden by later alterations and refacings and difficult to identify.

These changes were most common in the 17th and 18th centuries, as in the case of San Geremia, whose apse faces the Grand Canal. A little further along we see San Stae, with 18th century façade and the *Salute,* which marks its end and completes the count of churches along the Grand Canal.

Most of the other churches are to be found in little squares—*campi*—which you can discover later, behind the banks lined with palaces. These palaces are the glory of the city of the Doges.

Like the churches, they have been altered many times, and the sheer diversity of their styles is equally striking. But this very diversity, through its harmonies and discords, makes up what Elie Faure calls "the Venetian Symphony".

That is the thing one must hear, before gazing at the images formed by its palaces. The water laps at the mossy stones. Gondolas bob between the mooring-posts, which often bear the arms of their owners. Hallways afford a glimpse of damp flagstones. Above them, brick and marble are wedded, used in alternate panels. Gothic windows, arcades and facades tower over balconies of white stone.

But rarely does one see a silhouette. When evening comes, not a single light is to be seen in these facades. The palaces lie sunk in darkness like a stage setting after the play is over.

Yet each one has its story to tell. Who could tell it, uncover the treasures enclosed within those somber walls?

Here, near San Geremia, is Ca' Labia, where Tiepolo painted his allegorical works. A little further on is the Palazzo Correr-Contarini, called Ca' dei Cuori—the House of the Hearts. On the opposite bank are homes dating from the 16th century: Dorigo Giovanelli, with its huge four-bay windows, and Ca' Correr, whose collections were the nucleus of the museum of that name.

Facing San Marcuola—one stop further on by *vaporetto*—is the Fondaco dei Turchi, once the headquarters of the Turkish merchants, built in a Veneto-Byzantine style in the 17th century. A wide gallery forming a quay made it possible to unload merchandise here. Today the building houses the Museum of Natural History.

On the other bank stands the Palazzo Vendramin—Calergi, dating from the 16th century. It has a façade of gray stone with twin windows, in a style of austere harmony. It was here on 3rd February 1883, that Wagner died.

Two centuries earlier, in 1686, another musician was born not far from here in the palace which bears his name. Benedetto Marcello was one of the composers of the Golden Age in Venice. Further on, on the right bank just past the San Stae stop, is Ca' Pesaro, built by Longhena, like so many other palaces of the 17th century. Today it contains the Museum of Modern Art. And one more stop on the *vaporetto* brings you to one of the most fascinating palaces on the Grand Canal, Ca' d'Oro, the Golden House.

From the Ca' d'Oro to the Rialto

The Ca' d'Oro is the epitome of a Venetian palace of the 15th century. Above the arcaded gallery looking out over the Grand Canal rise two tiers of blind arches in the Gothic style surmounted by the quadrifoil motifs so characteristic of Venetian art, giving the palace an air of matchless grace. The gilding and polychrome work of its façade gave the building the name Ca' d'Oro. It was built at the beginning of the 15th century by Matteo Raverti and the brothers Buon in a style combining the Byzantinism of the lower gallery with the flamboyant Gothic of the upper galleries. These adaptations, common in Venice, make a composite architectural style the expression of an elegance and preciosity without becoming affected. It never peters out in pointless embellishment, as is the case with so many churches.

12

Left and opposite: two views of the famous Ca' d'Oro, the epitome of a 15th century Venetian palace.

You will need to make another trip to the Ca' d'Oro to learn something of the interior of a patrician house of the Golden Age of Venice and at the same time to see the Franchetti collection which is displayed here. There are two entrances, according to local custom, one from the canal and visible from the *vaporetto,* the other from the nearby *calle* by a sculptured gateway giving access to an interior courtyard with a marble staircase open to the sky. A well with a well-head in pink Verona marble is the work of Bartolomeo Buon. The coats of arms over the gateway were executed by Raverti.

Inside there are some outstanding works of art, a *Venus* by Titian, decked in pearls, a *St. Sebastian* by Mantegna, the *Annunciation and Death of the Virgin Mary* by Carpaccio, *Madonnas* by Cima and Le Perugin and another *Venus* by Paris Bordone.

But in the meantime, having anticipated this visit which is not to be missed, let us continue along the waterway, passing other palaces of equal elegance: Ca' Sag and Ca' Matteotti (18th century), Ca' da Mosto, a residence and warehouse of the 13th century extended upwards in the 17th century. Opposite these noble dwellings is the *Pescheria,* the Fishmarket, rebuilt in 1507, near which a very busy market is thronged every day by Venetians doing their shopping.

The Palazzo Camerlenghi on the quay of the *Pescheria* is the next point to visit. Built in

13

In the Rialto quarter stands the celebrated "Fondaco dei Tedeschi", once indeed the "Warehouse of the German Merchants" but today the Central Post Office. Right: the San Samuele stop on the Grand Canal. This fine picture captures one of the many charming aspects of Venice.

a Lombard style in the 16th century for the use of the financial officials *(camerlenghi),* it also housed a prison. Opposite stands the headquarters of the German merchants, the *Bondaco dei Tedeschi.* It has an interior courtyard and its façade along the Grand Canal was once adorned with frescoes by Giorgione.

The banks of the Grand Canal are here joined by the Rialto Bridge, the center of a quarter which was, and still is in part, the very heart of Venice. In the 13th century the busy traffic between the two banks necessitated a a wooden drawbridge. It was altered and restored in the course of succeeding centuries but in the end it collapsed under the weight of the crowd which gathered to see the entourage of the Marchioness of Ferrara.

When the senate organised a competition to obtain the best design for a stone bridge, Antonio da Ponte was declared the winner and built the bridge in 1588. The centre of the bridge is covered by shops between two covered galleries. Despite its architectural daring, its critics find it lacking in elegance.

From Bridge to Bridge

On the other side of the Rialto Bridge, on both sides of the Grand Canal, stretch quays, la Riva del Vin on the left and la Riva del Carbon on the right. Onto them lead extremely busy *calli,* thronged on the left by

shoppers from the nearby market and on the right by tourists coming from St. Mark's. Here and there are restaurants with terraces which make it possible to dine without missing any of the vivid spectacle or its splendid setting.

The Grand Canal widens out between the sumptuous palaces which succeed the quays: the Palazzo Dolfin-Manin, the home of the last Doge and with a 16th century façade by Sansovino, one of the great Venetian architects; and the Palazzi Loredan and Farsetti, built in the 13th century but much altered. Still on the right bank there is the Palazzo Corner-Spinelli, an example of the Renaissance style.

On the opposite bank the Palazzo Papadopoli, a fine 16th century building, is well worth a visit, as are the Palazzo Bernardo in the Gothic style (once the residence of Francesco Sforza, Duke of Milan) and the elegant Palazzo Pisani-Moretta with painting by Veronese, Tiepolo and Piazzetta. Finally, after the Rio Foscari, come the Palazzo Foscari and the Palazzo Giustinian, where Richard Wagner composed part of "Tristan and Isolde".

Ca' Rezzonico is the name of the next *vaporetto* stop. It is also the name of a palace which richly repays a visit. It was begun in 1660 by Longhena and finished by Massari. A monumental gateway leads from the quay to a courtyard containing statues and the lantern of a galley. Then Massari's great

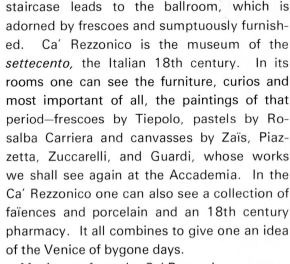

Views of the Grand Canal: below left, the most famous bridge in Venice, that of the Rialto. At the side is the Palazzo Cavalli.

staircase leads to the ballroom, which is adorned by frescoes and sumptuously furnished. Ca' Rezzonico is the museum of the *settecento,* the Italian 18th century. In its rooms one can see the furniture, curios and most important of all, the paintings of that period—frescoes by Tiepolo, pastels by Rosalba Carriera and canvasses by Zaïs, Piazzetta, Zuccarelli, and Guardi, whose works we shall see again at the Accademia. In the Ca' Rezzonico one can also see a collection of faïences and porcelain and an 18th century pharmacy. It all combines to give one an idea of the Venice of bygone days.

Moving on from the Ca' Rezzonico we come to the Palazzo Contarini, near the third bridge over the Grand Canal, that of the Accademia. This wooden bridge leads to the Accademia itself, that treasure-house of Venetian painting of the 15th to 18th centuries, to which we shall return later.

At the ponte dell'Accademia the Grand Canal completes its final bend and offers one a view of the lagoon, here called *Canale di San Marco.* On its ever-widening banks stands a double row of famous palaces: on the right the Palazzo Dario, built in the Lombard style and faced with rare marbles; on the left the Palazzo Cavalli and Corner della Ca' Grande, designed by Sansovino for the Queen of Cyprus and nowadays the prefecture, the Palazzo Gritti (now a hotel, like so many other palaces in this quarter), the Palazzo

17

Contarini-Fasan, in the Flamboyant Gothic style and, according to legend, the home of Desdemona, and finally Ca' Giustinian (15th century), which provides office accommodation for the Venice Biennale.

We have selected a number of palaces out of many. They are too numerous for us to mention all of them, all those palaces along the waterways where the noise of engines has replaced the songs of the gondoliers.

Opposite Ca' Giustinian, the familiar outline of Santa Maria della Salute and the buildings of the 18th century *Dogana* (customs house) mark the end of the Grand Canal.

The basilica of the Salute was built to commemorate the end of the plague of 1630. Constructed by Longhena, its octagonal shape is dominated by two huge domes. The interior offers the finest example of the baroque style to be seen in Venice. It contains outstanding works by Titian and Tintoretto, excellent Biblical scenes in the sacristy and the *Marriage Feast of Cana,* a large canvas by Tintoretto.

From the broad stairs which lead from the basilica down to the canal there is a view of the most exquisite scene in all Venice: the

In Venice everything is history, the city lives on its magnificent past, which still survives in its palaces, its memories, its works of art and the reconstructions so dear to Venetian hearts.

18

Palace of the Doges, the Piazzetta, the Molo, the Riva degli Schiavoni. At the San Marco Giardini stop the traveler steps ashore again to enter the very heart of the Most Serene Republic.

Memories treasured by all visitors to Venice: the restaurants on the Grand Canal and the humble vaporetto.

2. WATER AND STONE

Water and stone; the eternal and the ephemeral; the immutable and the mobile. These are the two images of Venice which contrast and merge. Where the white stone steps thrust into the water, the waves break and fall back in foam. The floating gondolas give a ceaseless lapping sound. Worm-eaten piles creak between stone and water. Pigeons peck at crumbs invisible to the eye. And the traveler daydreams on the shore of the lagoon.

It is one of the urban landscapes most celebrated by the arts, one of the finest the world has to show. Opposite us, over the silvery water, lies the dome and the campanile of San Giorgio, which according to the whims of the weather stands out sharply or is blurred. On the horizon islands and fields seem to float on the lagoon.

The quay, also called the Mole, was the place where the galleys used to berth. The pavement is of brick and stone, and two columns mark the entrance to an empire, La Piazzetta. And standing out against the sky, which the enormous but light building seems to set at defiance, one sees the Palace of the Doges, its pink façade set above its double row of small marble columns. These are

Left: glasswork and gondolas, well known Venetian products. In the background the buildings on the Point of the Dogana, where the Grand Canal enters the lagoon.

images which do not have their like elsewhere, and once seen, will never be forgotten.

Further on, in a tangle of pilasters and domes, can be seen the complex lacework of the basilica of St. Mark. There is more than a contrast, there is a positive antithesis between the severity of the palace and sheer exuberance of the church. At the front forming the boundary of the Piazzetta, the campanile stands out, like a challenge, from Sansovino's graceful loggia. And in front of St. Mark's is the piazza, the square which Napoleon said was the "finest drawing-room in Europe".

Such a sight makes an unforgettable impression on one's mind and defies adequate description. Seen through the milling crowds, the fluttering pigeons, the hordes of tourists, the picturesque seems to contend with the sublime and the everyday with the historical. From the Clock Tower the hours are struck by two bronze Moors. The Piazza San Marco is truly the heart of Venice.

The Basilica

The first basilica was started in 828 under Doge Partecipazio to provide a shrine for the relics of St. Mark the Evangelist brought from Alexandria by two mariners, Buono de Malamocco and Rustici de Torcello. It was consecrated in 832. All that remains of this early building is a few fragments of sculpture

BENEDIT U SQUI UENIT IN NOMINE DOMINI

St. Mark's: interior and stained glass window.

and some ancient cornices. It was burnt down in 976 in the course of a popular uprising against the Doge. His successor Orseolo started a new church two years later. Of this one can still see two arches at the base of the choir. Finally in 1063 the Doge Contarini built the third church in the Byzantine style. Construction went on well into the 15th century, notably the facing of the brick with marble and the crown of spires around the domes. As each successive architect used the style then in favor, St. Mark's, while oriental as a whole, shows trends and influences which are clearly Roman, Gothic, Tuscan, Lombard and so on. That is precisely why it has an irritating lack of style. The sheer accumulation of decoration seems to be intended to make good the lack of any precise architectural plan, and acts as a sort of mask for the building, which is completely hidden behind the size of the portals of the narthex and the forest of cupolas and spires which covers it!

The decoration of the central and side façades is equally noteworthy. And most important of all are the 13th century mosaics in the roof vaults of the narthex. With all the archaic flavor of Byzantine art they depict biblical scenes. In the gallery overlooking the narthex stand the magnificent horses of gilded bronze (Greek works of the 3rd century B.C.) brought back by the Venetians from the capture and pillage of Constantinople.

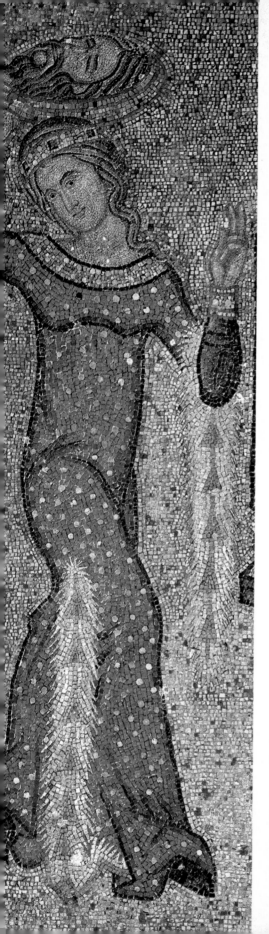

Left and center: two fine examples of 10th century Byzantine art in St. Mark's. Above: details of a portal of St. Mark's. Opposite: detail of external ironwork.

The exquisite mosaics in the façade of St. Mark's. Below: the clock tower which overlooks the ancient alleyways of the city.

The interior of the basilica is much more majestic than the exterior and makes an even more profound impression on the visitor. From the half-light of the three naves open chapels rich in marbles and bronzes: the baptistery with reliefs and mosaics showing scenes from the life of St. John the Baptist (note especially the "Dance of Salome"; the Zen chapel and that of the Treasury with magnificent works in silver and gold.

The choir, placed above the crypt, contains a high altar under which is buried the body of St. Mark. Behind this is the famous *Pala d'Oro,* an altarpiece adorned with enamels and precious stones which is greatly admired, though more for its intrinsic than its artistic value: 1300 fine pearls, 1100 precious stones (rubies, saphires, emeralds, amethysts etc.) were used in the settings of enamels showing biblical scenes and the portraits of saints. This masterpiece of the goldsmith's art was commissioned in Constantinople in the 10th century by Doge Orseolo, then extended and embellished in Venice in the centuries that followed. Despite its value, which is beyond calculation, or rather because of it, this marvel bears impressive witness to a certain view of the church. It also testifies to the pride of Venice, served in such a masterly way by its artists and craftsmen.

Several of the Doges have tombs in the basilica and under the narthex, very near the palace which saw their days of glory.

The façade of the Palace of the Doges facing the lagoon. Right: statuettes and dome, views of a staircase, a room and the courtyard.

The Palace of the Doges

The palace is beyond any doubt one of the most amazing architectural successes to be seen anywhere in the world. In this "upside down palace", as somebody has called it, the compact but light-seeming mass of the building is supported only by a double row of marble columns! This miracle of architecture is made even more striking by the severity and simplicity of its lines. Whether, seen from the lagoon, it sometimes seems drowned in mist, or, viewed from the piazzetta, it shines out in the brilliant sunlight which brings out so well

the pink and white of its marbles, the Palace of the Doges combines nobility with beauty. It is one of those perfect works which the mind of man creates for its own enrichment.

The huge inner courtyard, built in plainer style, contains a well and the Staircase of the Giants, designed by A. Rizzo and flanked by colossal statues of Mars and Neptune by Sansovino.

The palace served a number of different purposes: it was the seat of the government, it accommodated the private apartments of the Doges and, under the roof there were prisons, the famous "Leads" described from

personal experience by Casanova. On the other side of the rio spanned by the Bridge of Sighs is another prison, known as the "Wells".

The interior of the palace has much to interest the visitor—the majestic Senate Chamber, Council Chambers and Election Chamber, together with the even more fascinating pictures which adorn them. The palace was the residence of the Doges who guided the destiny of Venice, here was acted out its history as extolled by the canvasses of Tintoretto, Veronese, Palma the Younger and Bassano. In these works both Christian saints and pagan gods are associated with the glories of Venice. The masterpiece which outshines all others is the "Paradise" (82 feet by 26), painted by Tintoretto at the age of seventy!

The Piazzetta

From the front of the palace of the Doges the Piazzetta extends right down to the lagoon. It is dominated by two free-standing columns brought from Acre in the 13th century and set up on stepped bases decorated with sculptures, the stone of which has been worn away by the feet of countless generations of tourists.

On the capitals stand two figures which symbolise Venice: the statue of Theodore, first patron saint of the city, and a winged lion which must originally have been a Chinese

chimaera with added wings to turn it into the symbol of St. Mark the Evangelist.

The Piazzetta is the ideal place for understanding and admiring Venice. On one side one sees the lagoon with its skyline of domes, campaniles and gondolas rocking gently on the waters. On the other side stands the façade of the palace, the crowds and the pigeons, the basilica and the Clock Tower.

On the other side of the Piazzetta stands the Libreria Sansoviniana. This building, with its two rows of arches, was begun in the years 1536-1554 by Sansovino and finished in 1588 by Scamozzi. It houses the library founded in 1468 by Cardinal Bessarion, now containing 500,000 volumes and 3,000 incunabula. It also contains an archaeological museum open to the public.

Sansovino was also the architect responsible for the delightful *"loggietta"* leading up to the campanile. The original campanile, built in the 13th and 14th centuries, collapsed suddenly in 1902. It was rebuilt in accordance with the original plans from 1905 to 1912 and a lift was installed to take people to the top, where there is a marvellous view of the city and the lagoon.

The Piazza

On the other side of the *loggietta,* in front of the cathedral, lies the huge quadrilateral of the Piazza San Marco, along which stand

the Procuratie, formerly the offices of the Procurators of St Mark. On the side where the campanile stands are the *Procuratie Nuove* and on the other side the *Procuratie Vecchie* (15th and 16th centuries) and the Clock Tower, where two Moors strike the hours near a statue of the Virgin.

In former times the church of San Gimigniano, built by Sansovino, also stood in the square. It was demolished by Napoleon so that he could close off the square with the Neo-Classical *Procuratie Novissime* containing ballrooms and banqueting rooms of a grandeur in keeping with the Second Empire. Nowadays this building houses the Museo Corror, where one can see sculptures by Canova, arms, armor, robes worn by the Doges, models of galleys, portraits and documents, all dating from the days of the Most Serene Republic. There is also a notable collection

The sights of the Piazza San Marco which tourists never tire of: the galleries with shops full of interesting things to buy, the terrace of the famous Café Florian and the local pigeons.

of paintings from the period up to the 16th century: Antonello da Messina, C. Tura, Giovanni Bellini and the celebrated "Two Courtesans" by Carpaccio. All this is a superb evocation of the past and puts the finishing touches to the vivid impressions left in one's mind by the Piazzetta and the Piazza.

Under the arcades along the sides of the Piazza are famous shops and cafés. There is a plaque commemorating Wagner. In the "Café Florian" tourists are shown a Chinese glass-painting which has looked down on gatherings of writers and poets for generations. And for decades the orchestra of the café has been playing Viennese waltzes of Richard Strauss.

Set within the rigid framework of its arcades, the square looks like an enormous playground. Tourists stroll about, children scamper, pigeons flutter into the air. But, fearsome thought, it is forbidden under pain of fines to "picknick, play cards, make music (no doubt the cafés are exempt) and lie on the ground"!

The Lagoon Front

Here and there along the Piazzetta there are quays leading to the lagoon. This was the place where in days gone by, galleys used to land. The mole used to be fortified with towers and ramparts. Nowadays there is a little garden fringing the quay to the west, the

37

By way of the Ponte della Paglia, used each year by hundreds of thousands of visitors (and much frequented in the Renaissance period, as one can see from the painting on the right), one reaches the "Riva degli Schiavoni" or "Quay of the Esclavonians".

only stretch of green in the center of Venice.
However, Venice manages quite well without
more.

To the east of the Piazzetta the Ponte della
Paglia (1360) decorated with fine sculptures,
marks the beginning of the Riva degli Schiavoni—the Quay of the Slavs. It bears this
name because in bygone centuries sailors
from the Dalmatian coast (then called
"Sclavonia") went ashore there.

From the Ponte della Paglia one has a view
of the Bridge of Sighs, which links the Palace
of the Doges with the prisons on the other side
of the rio.

The Riva of the Schiavoni is more than 500
yards long and faces the wide basin of the
lagoon and the island of San Giorgio Maggiore. This is the district which abounds in
large hotels, cafés with terraces, souvenir-
shops and painters who do you a portrait in a

Left: the Bridge of Sighs, best viewed from the Ponte della Paglia. Also two street painters, particularly numerous in Venice.

few minutes. It is also the tourists' favorite place for a walk, and has all the busy, bustling traffic you would expect in a city. Several *vaporetto* lines have their landing-stages in the Riva, not only for trips to the Grand Canal, but also to San Giorgio, the Lido and more distant islands. Gondoliers ply for hire there.

Most of the large hotels are in former palaces converted in the 18th and 19th centuries. The most famous, the Hotel Danieli, is the former *Albergo Reale,* founded in the 19th century in a Gothic palace which was also the residence of the French Ambassador. George Sand and Musset conducted their tempestuous love affairs there, and a large number of famous figures have stayed there in the past hundred years.

A little further along is the chapel of the Pietà, an orphanage where Vivaldi was musical director from 1705 to 1740: the art of music also produced some of its greatest masterpieces in Venice.

3. THE LEFT BANK

In previous chapters we have pointed out the favorite places in the City of the Doges for visiting tourists, especially those in a hurry. They are the most famous sights, but there is more to Venice. It is a large city of 350,000 inhabitants which lives entirely on tourism. On the mainland it is flanked by the urban center of Mestre and the industrial complex of Maghera. More of these later.

The city itself, built on 118 islands joined by 400 bridges and crossed by 177 canals, is divided into two unequal parts by the course of the Grand Canal. This course is in the shape of an inverted S, the loops (north and south) also being extremely rich in monuments and associations with the past. When the city prospered and expanded, fringe areas sprang up, inhabited by craftsmen, workers and small businessmen.

For administrative purposes the city is divided into 6 districts *(sestieri)*, half on the left bank of the Grand Canal and half on the right. In this chapter and the next we shall attempt to identify their countless points of interest.

One should not leave Venice without walking through those amazing *calli* (streets), those *sottoportegi* (lanes and passageways), which are some of them less than a yard wide. Nor should one leave without having lingered on the *campi,* leaned over the narrow *rii* or crossed those hump-backed bridges which preserve the city from the scourge of wheeled traffic !

The three *sestieri* of the left bank are San Marco on the bend of the Grand Canal, Cannaregio to the North and Castello to the East. In the streets of the center arrows indicate various tours on foot. It is pleasant to heed them at first, then forget them and go where fancy takes you. As the poet Henri de Régnier wrote: "Let us lose our way in Venice".

Sestieri di San Marco

The best known of these tiny, flagstone-paved streets is the *Merceria* which leads from San Marco to the Rialto. It starts near the Clock Tower and winds between two rows of little shops which sell everything under the sun. Here you can find all kind of goods made elsewhere, plus the products of local craftsmen, from souvenir gondolas to gondoliers' hats. The tourist who walks from St Mark's to the Rialto bridge or from the *Caffé Florian to* the *Ristorante Florida* has no lack of things to spend his lire on.

As we walk we come across interesting churches. San Salvatore has some paintings by Titian and Bellini and the tomb of the Doge Vernier by Sansovino, who also built the 17th century façade.

The Merceria leads to the *Campo San Bartolomeo.* In the evenings it is the meeting-

place of crowds of Venetians who linger there deep in conversation until night falls. In the neighboring *calli* there is a profusion of little bars and *trattorie* where you can drink *cappucini* or enjoy an icecream. On the Campo San Bartolomeo there is a monument to Carlo Goldoni, the Molière of 18th century Venice. The church was rebuilt in the same period. It contains four organ-panels painted by Sebastiano del Piombo.

In this brief portrait of Venice there is not sufficient space to mention all the churches which are worthy of note. You will come across them in your walks, and we will limit ourselves to mentioning the outstanding ones, whether because of their architecture or the work of art which they contain.

Every *campo* has its church, particularly in the western part of the *sestiere San Marco* enclosed by the Grand Canal. From the portico near the Procuratie the Salizzada San Moisè leads to a maze of busy little streets containing banks, offices and large hotels. A *salizzada* is a street paved by *salizo,* a local stone. The church of San Moisè stands in the *campo,* a 17th century building with a particularly ornate Baroque façade. The little bridge, moored gondolas, the rio flowing into the Grand Canal, all make a picturesque scene, as does the nearby Rio Orseolo and its fleet of gondolas.

Further on we come to another Baroque church, Santa Maria del Giglio (pictures by Tintoretto), and San Stefano, built in the 14th and 15th centuries in the Gothic style. You can reach the Ponte dell'Accademia and the right bank via the vast Campo Morosini and San Vitale.

Those who are fond of music will want to visit the Palazzo Pisani, formerly the residence

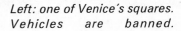
Left: one of Venice's squares. Vehicles are banned.

of a rich Venetian family and now housing the Benedetto Marcello Conservatory of Music. In its museum you can see the desk and baton used by Wagner at his last concert in 1882.

The Teatro de la Fenice, another focal point of Venetian musical life, has a rather dull façade facing a little square. It was opened in 1792 and partly burned down in 1836. The site was too cramped to allow space for a more effective reconstruction. The theater comprises two groups of buildings. The one facing the canal seats 1500 people in period decor—gilt frames, wood and stucco sculptures and four tiers of seating.

Amongst the many palaces in this once aristocratic district the Palazzo Querini, near the ancient church of San Zulian, is worthy of note. It houses the collections donated to the city by Count Querini: furniture, porcelain, arms and armor, paintings from the principal periods of the Venetian School. It is also worth taking a look at the Ca' Contarini "dal Bovolo", built at the end of the 15th century in the Gothic style with a tower with a curious spiral gallery.

Opposite: a photograph emphasizes that Venice is truly a part of Italy.

47

Exterior and interior of the La Fenice theatre. Below: the church of San Zaccaria.

From San Zaccaria to San Pietro in Castello

East of the Palace of the Doges and behind the Riva degli Schiavoni lies a district which is quite extensive and extremely diverse, the *sestiere* of Castello, which takes in the eastern point of Venice—the tail of the "sword-fish"—as far as the gardens of Santa Elena. The western part of this area is very rich in churches and intersected by picturesque little canals which reflect the image of ancient houses. There are some narrow streets at right-angles to the Riva degli Schiavoni which abound in restaurants and *trattorie*. Past the *sottoportego* of San Zaccaria leading onto the quay you come to the campo and church of San Zaccaria, one of the most ancient in the city. After the Renaissance façade, take a look at the fine Gothic choir and crypt, the last remaining parts of the 9th century church. The brick campanile belonged to a Benedictine monastery built earlier than the church. Amongst the other churches we can single out for special attention Santa Maria Formosa (1492), San Giorgio dei Greci, built by the Greek Orthodox community at the end of the 15th century and completed in the 16th century in the Renaissance style, with an iconostasis, adorned with marbles and paintings in the Greco-Byzantine style.

We must mention particularly the church of San Giorgio degli Schiavoni, which is a veritable gallery of Carpaccio paintings illustrating the lives of Saints George, Tryphon and Jerome, protectors of Dalmatia.

At the end of the Riva degli Schiavoni one comes to the Rio del Arsenale and the Naval Museum. It contains Venetian naval exhibits and the remains of the last "Bucentoro", or state barge of the Doges, destroyed in 1797. The *fondamento* leads to the entrance to the Arsenal which is flanked by two towers and adorned with sculptures. Two of the stone lions there were brought from Athens by Morosini, the conqueror of the Turks.

Founded in the 12th century, the Arsenal soon became a naval shipyard famous all over

Europe. A huge dock was opened to the East and fortified by a crenellated wall which still stands. The *vaporetto* from Fondamento Nuove crosses the entrance basin, but most of the yards are deserted and the buildings falling into decay. A few naval units still keep alive a hint of the glories of the past.

Further to the east, the quay now called the Riva dei Martiri leads to the via Garibaldi, one of the few thoroughfares in Venice actually called a street. It is in fact a wide, busy street crowded with shops and business houses and it leads to the Fondamento Sant' Ana and the *calli* which intersect between the walls of the Arsenal and the Canale di San Pietro. This is a district which one simply must see if one is to understand the Venice over-looked by the tourists, even if the impression one has is often a little astringent. Life goes on in these houses despite the dilapidation of their walls, but the ground floors are mostly sordid hovels. In former times craftsmen

lived and worked there, and the place echoed to the sounds of forges and workshops. In the Campo Ruga and the Campo di Figareto washing hangs on the balconies of former palaces. This is the dark side of Venice, but it is certainly not without beauty.

Two bridges over the Canale di San Pietro link this district with the island of the same name, which is mostly inhabited by fishermen. The Bishops of Venice set up their palace there in 775 and built a church which was the cathedral of Venice until 1807. In that year the Bishops—made Patriarchs in 1451 by the Pope—left their palace, which became a military barracks.

The church underwent several alterations in the course of the centuries. The façade one sees today is built in Istrian stone and dates from 1596. The interior in the shape of a Latin cross contains the throne which legend says was that of St. Peter at Antioch. In the presbytery there is an urn containing relics of

St. Laurence. Infront of the church a grass-covered campo fringes the canal.

To the south of the island of San Pietro in Castello lies another island, that of Sant' Elena. It has sports grounds and gardens which continue on the other side of the canal with palaces and the building of the International Art Exhibition, which is the setting for the Venice Biennale.

It can be reached by the "Giardini" *vaporetto* stop. The next stop, "Sant' Elena", is the last one before the Lido.

The Northern Shore

A long, straight quay, the "Fondamento Nuove", stretches to the north of Venice opposite the island of San Michele, the cemetery of Venice whose black cypresses stand out sharply against the sky.

From the "Fondamento Nuove" you can take *vaporetti* to the islands of the lagoon. Particularly on days when the weather is poor it is the coldest part of the city, swept by north winds.

At the back there are many churches and a few palaces: San Francesco della Vigna, built by Sansovino and Palladio in the 16th century, is rich in sculptures. Most interesting is San Giovanni e Paolo, also called San Zanipolo and known as "the Pantheon of the Doges" Several Doges of the Mocenigo family are buried there, as is Doge Andrea Vendramin,

in a tomb designed by Lombardo and considered a key work of Venetian funerary art of the 15th century. Admirals, captains and scholars are interred in the church.

Begun in the 12th century by the Dominicans, San Giovanni e Paolo was completed in the 15th. Its high Gothic nave ends in a

Above: view of the island of San Michele, Venice's cemetery. Opposite: Verrocchio's well-known statue of Bartolomeo Colleoni.

52

A picturesque trattoria like so many in Venice — the "Trattoria of the Three Hunchbacks". Below: a shopping street in the Rialto district.

Gothic apse, and the façade has Renaissance features. The tombs of the Doges Jacopo and Lorenzo Tiepolo can be seen there.

To the left of the church stands the former Scuola di San Marco founded in 1260. Its marble Renaissance façade dates from the end of the 15th century.

In the middle of the *Campo* is the magnificent equestrian statue of the condottiere Bartolomeo Colleoni designed by Verrochio (1481-1488) and cast in bronze by Leopardi.

Further to the north, near the Fondamento Nuove is the church of the Jesuits, Santa Maria del Rosario, a Baroque building constructed from 1714 to 1729. Its interior, shaped like a Latin cross, has a chair with baldacchino, a high altar with twisted columns and magnificent floral decorations in grey with various marbles and stucco. The ceiling has frescoes by Tiepolo.

On the other side of the canal, which is here much wider than when it passes the Ca' d'Oro, the district of Cannaregio extends as far as the *stazione* over a series of *rii* parallel to the shore. The rio of Cannaregio is the most important there. It has a stone bridge of three arches and joins the Grand Canal at the Campo San Geremia. La Lista de Spagna leading from San Geremia to the stazione is a very busy street with many hotels, restaurants and shops of all kinds. It is the opposite tourist pole of Venice, near the railroad terminus.

53

Gondolas, gondolas, gondolas...

On later pages some of Venice's 400 bridges.

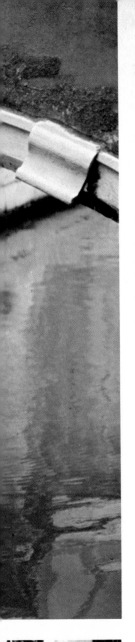

Views of the canals.

4. THE RIGHT BANK OF THE GRAND CANAL

The right bank, like that on the left, has three administrative districts: San Polo, Santa Croce and Dorsoduro, which takes in the whole southern part of the city.

To the west lie the quays, the anchorages and the dock railroad system, which links up with the main railroad network at the Ponte de la Libertà. One of these railroads passes south of Dorsoduro to the quays of Zattere, but is concerned only with goods traffic.

Large docks accommodate cargo and passenger vessels, for Venice is also the center of a network of shipping lanes and a port of call for cruises. On the other side of the docks an artificial island has been built to park the thousands of cars forced to stop at the very threshold of Venice, where wheeled transport is banned.

From the Scalzi to San Rocco

Let us return to our point of departure, the "Ferrovia" stop and, opposite the church of the same name, the Bridge of the Scalzi. For the pedestrian it gives access to the western bend of the Grand Canal. It is a replica of the other bank, with little narrow streets, solitary *campi,* churches and palaces. But the throng of tourists is less dense than near the Merceria, and the traveler is better able to see the ancient face of Venice. It is also rather more aristocratic district than those on the left bank, with wider streets and some more spacious palaces. There is no lack of churches. San Giacomo dell'Orio was built in the 8th century and rebuilt in the 13th. It has Byzantine, Gothic and Renaissance elements. San Cassino, which has a belfry in the Venetian Gothic style, was also altered in the 17th century. San Silvestro stands near the Grand Canal. Sant' Aponal has parts which date from the 11th, 15th and 16th centuries. Finally San Polo, standing in the large *campo* which bears its name. This church has a Gothic portal and 12th century marble lions. The brick belfry dates from the same period.

Near the Rialto is San Giacomo di Rialto with its portico of columns. It is probably the oldest church in Venice. Not far away, by the side of the canal are the great markets of Venice: the *Erberia,* selling fruit and vegetables, the *Casaria* selling cheese and other milk products, and the *Pescheria* selling sea-food. A walk around the markets is always interesting and instructive. It enables us to feel the pulse of the daily life of a city.

But on this bend of the Grand Canal two visits are highly recommended, one to Santa Maria dei Frari, the church of the Franciscans, and one to the church and Scuola of San Rocco full of magnificent works from the Golden Age of Venice, including some by Titian and Tintoretto.

The basilica of Santa Maria Gloria dei Frari

Portal of the basilica of Santa Maria Gloria dei Frari: it has a vitality and grandeur which are typically Renaissance. Inside, canvasses by Titian and Bellini, a statue by Donatello.

is one of the most interesting in Venice. In the sobriety and amplitude of its three naves, in the elegance of its Gothic choir it shows true religious character, that is, feeling and greatness which are often lacking in the church-palaces of the Renaissance. It owes its existence to the Franciscan Friars Minor who replaced the first church of the order by this Gothic basilica, whose marble work contrasts strikingly with the brick. The portal opens onto a *campo* by a narrow *rio.* The whole complex makes a picture of entrancing harmony.

The richness of the church is equalled by its nobility. Funerary monuments adorn the side naves and various chapels, including the tombs of Titian, Canova, Monteverdi and several Doges: Foscari, Dandolo and Pesaro. Over the high altar there is a magnificent canvas by Titian, "The Assumption" (1518). In the transept chapels you can see a "Virgin

and Child" by Giovanni Bellini (1488) and a statue of St. John the Baptist by Donatello. The choir has 124 carved and inlaid stalls, including some very fine work.

The former Convent of the Franciscans now houses the State Archives—15 million volumes arranged in 300 rooms. Theses documents record a thousand years of Venetian history.

Not for away, in another *campo,* is the church of San Rocco, built in the 15th century but with a façade dating from the 18th. It contains pictures of the Venetian School, notably Tintoretto, and Renaissance decorations. But it is really in the Scuola di San Rocco that you see Tintoretto's masterpieces—about fifty vast canvasses and painted deilings. These make San Rocco a veritable Tintoretto gallery, an important fact when you consider that he, with Titian, was the greatest painter of the Venetian School.

The "Pescheria", one of Venice's markets, like the "Erberia" and "Casaria". Below: the church of San Rocco, with work by Tintoretto.

San Rocco and the Tintoretto Masterpieces

He was called Jacopo Robusti and lived in Venice from about 1518 to 1594. The son of a dyer, he was hence called Tintoretto (from *tintore* meaning dyer). It is said that the dye-vats he saw as a child must have given him his awareness of colors. His father entrusted him to the greatest painter of the age, Titian. But so great was the pupil's talent that the master took offense. Tintoretto had to leave the studio and pursue his studies alone. However, he retained his admiration for the master who had rejected him. Some time later he wrote on the wall of his room the words which summed up his ideal: "Michelangelo's drawing and Titian's colors."

For his first works he asked only the cost of the paints. Whilst Titian was working for princes and nobles, Tintoretto had to content himself with working for religious congregations less well endowed with wealth, but he

67

put all his fire and faith into his paintings. He got married and lived a peaceful, life with his wife Faustina and his daughter Marietta, herself an artist and musician, who died at the age of thirty.

In a competition in which Veronese and two other painters participated he won the commission for the Scuola di San Rocco. He worked there for a quarter of a century, carrying out his marvellous illustrations of biblical scenes. Learning much from the works of Michelangelo which he saw on a visit to Rome, he gave his own compositions the same sense of space. His figures are composed with a breathtaking sense of movement magnified by the interplay of light and shade, the contrasting colors and the astonishing beauty of the treatment.

Most important of all, Tintoretto's evocation of the great moments in sacred history brings the settings and background of the dramatic events totally up to date. Whether it is the *Annunciation,* the *Nativity,* or the *Flight into Egypt,* he sweeps aside the received ideas about the figures and the backgrounds. He varies the views and adds life to the main scenes by subsidiary motifs. One might be tempted to say that Tintoretto was the first film-producer in Italian art!

At the end of your visit you will see his great *Crucifixion* on the wall of the *Albergo.* This is not only the most masterly work in the group, it is one of the most beautiful canvasses in the world. Never has this key theme of religious art found such a dramatically compelling expression, nor has it ever given rise to such as a strict composition, in which, in this case, Tintoretto's art approaches musical feeling. This painting is a symphony. Its Christ on the cross as the central motif, the great empty space where the thieves' crosses are yet to be set up, the groups of sorrowful figures at the foot of the cross on each side, balancing each other out, the trumpets of the soldiers and horsemen.

The Accademia: The Venetian School

Tintoretto, the dyer's son, in his rich and abundant works, marked the end of the great age of Venetian painting. After him the rich vein was exhausted in the 17th century. It revived in different forms in the 18th, but certainly without any continuity with the Golden Age of the Renaissance.

We must turn back to its origins, to the time when painting broke away from the Byzantine tradition. When the great destiny of Venice began to emerge clearly, a school of painting was formed which was to flourish throughout the 15th and 16th centuries.

We can trace its development and wonder at its achievements in Venice's Academy of Fine Arts. Standing near the bridge which bears its name, the Accademia is a gallery of modest size but immense quality. It contains

a number of canvasses by other Italian schools (Florence and Padua) and by foreign masters. But the vast majority of its works covers all the periods of Venetian painting up to and including the 18th century.

The first rooms are devoted to the Primitives, heirs of the Byzantine tradition, with their Virgins and Christs set against backgrounds of gold. The Vivarinis (two brothers and a son of one of the latter) and Crivelli (1430-1493), who did little work in Venice, initiated the school. But the new school only began to gather strength with the Bellinis. Jacopo (1400-1470) decisively abandoned the Gothic style. His elder son, Gentile (1429-1507), was an official painter and even Ambassador of the Republic of Venice. His brother Giovanni, called Giambellino (1430-1516), was the first painter to develop the sensuous charm of the Venetian School. The *Accademia* has a wonderful series of *Virgins* whose youthful features, pouting lips and dreamy gaze are shown against backgrounds of intense color. There is also a fair-haired Mary Magdalene with child-like grace, brightly-hued draperies, pensive pose and restrained gestures. It is a painting to delight the eyes and the mind of the beholder.

It has a fine portrait of a young man by Lorenzo Lotto (1480-1556). Against the harmonious dark colors of the rest, the black and white of the hands and face stand out in sharp contrast. There are two remarkable

The frescoes in the "Room of the Four Doors" in the Palace of the Doges are by Tintoretto.

canvasses by Giorgione: the *Old Woman,* which reminds one of Goya, and the *Tempest.* But with Vittorio Carpaccio (1450-1525) the 16th century begins. The painter of San Giorgio degli Schiavoni is represented here by a whole room devoted to the legend of Saint Ursula. It is a series of large canvasses with magnificent imagery in which legend and realism combine to produce a kind of dramatic poem. The careful accuracy of the detail, the sense of scenic animation make it (though in quite a different way from Tintoretto's) a visual story imbued with poetry. Everything is realistic but also magic, fairy-like.

In the large central room and the one next to it can be seen works of 16th century masters: Tintoretto, including notably his *Removal of the Body of St. Mark,* illustrating the famous scene in Alexandria, the great compositions of Veronese (1528-1588), certainly remarkable but lacking the greatness of Tintoretto and the originality of Carpaccio. Finally there is an admirable Titian, his last *Pieta,* a skilful work with warm, muted colors and that irradiation of light which makes Titian the Rembrandt of Venice. Tiziano Vecellio, born about 1477, learned his art in Venice, but the city has few of his works. He worked at Ferrara, Mantua, Rome and Ausburg, at the court of Charles V. In later years he returned to Venice and died in 1576 during an outbreak of the Plague, aged almost a hundred.

We deal later with the 18th century painters —Zuccarelli, Zaïs, Longhi, Tiepolo and the *vedute* painters, Guardi and Canaletto—though they too are only thinly represented in Venice.

The Point of the Dogana.

Point of the Dogana and the Quays of Zattere

Those interested in modern paintings will find the Gougenheim Collection (open to the public in summer) works by Picasso, Matisse, Klee, Chagall etc. Near the Salute there is also the Pinacoteca Manfrediana and in the nearby church of San Giorgio a *Last Supper* by Tintoretto, rendered with a sharply tragic atmosphere.

On the other side of the Salute the quay continues to the Point of the *Dogana,* built in the 17th century. From there one can get to the quays of Zattere which extend along the canal opposite the Island of Giudecca. It is a replica of the Fondamenta Nuove, but the other way round, facing South. Zattere has a delightful position. There are several churches on the quay: Santo Spirito, with a façade in the Lombard style, the 18th century Santa Maria del Rosario (or degli Jesuiti) with canvasses by Tintoretto and frescoes by Tiepolo. Near the latter church, on the façade of the La Calcina Hotel, a plaque commemorates the fact that John Ruskin lived there in 1877. Ruskin's works are full of passionate enthusiasm for Venice.

Opposite Zattere lies the island of Giudecca, in effect a suburb of Venice. It has some interesting churches: the Redentore, built by Palladio from 1577 to 1592, and Santa Eu-

fonia, whose origins go back to the 9th century. The island mainly contains industrial and residential areas.

More familiar to tourists is the island of San Giorgio opposite St. Mark's. This island also forms part of Venice. From the top of its campanile there is splendid view of the City.

The church was built by Palladio in 1566 and finished in the 17th century by Scamozzi. It has paintings by Carpaccio and Tintoretto, especially a *Last Supper* with an innovatory touch—the view is from above down, onto the table around which Christ and his disciples are gathered.

In the square in front of the church, paved with flagstones set out in geometrical paterns,

San Giorgio Maggiore. Below: a monastery on the island.

is the entrance to the Cini Foundation, where one can attend exhibitions of, and discussions on, art. It is in a building formerly a Benedictine convent. The cloisters by Palladio and Longhena have been restored. The former refectory has become a conference hall. An open-air theater has been set up in the gardens to the south of the island.

73

General view of Venice and its setting.

5. THE ISLANDS AND THE LAGOON

However great the attractions of Venice itself, one must devote one day to the islands of the lagoon. First Murano, Burano and Torcello, which are to Venice what Fiesole is to Florence and Tivoli to Rome.

Excursions by boat can be made from the Riva degli Schiavoni, but it is better to use the regular services, for which the landing-stage is on the Fondamenta Nuove. They leave the visitor greater freedom to use his time as he thinks fit.

Crossing the lagoon gives one the opportunity of getting to know both the lagoon and the islands which were the starting point of Venice's history. In the course of the centuries they were settled by refugees from the Roman towns of the coast, Tarvisium (Treviso) and Altinum (Altino). Roman reliefs of the second century on the pillars of the church in Murano bear witness to these early days. This basilica of SS. Maria e Donato was founded in the 7th century. It was rebuilt in the 12th century in the Byzantine style of Ravenna. The mosaics of the Virgin on the vault of the apse, with their gold background, date from this period. The exterior is remarkable for its apse, composed of a double gallery of molded arches on small elegant columns.

Left: a view of the lagoon. Below: a view of Murano.

Left: the rio of Murano. Above: specimens of Venice's celebrated glasswork.

The Murano Glassworks

Murano is biult on five islands separated by wide canals and joined by bridges. At one time it was a resort where Venetian nobles built summer residences with gardens full of rare plants. But from the 13th century onwards frequent fires in the city led to the crafts which used furnaces being banned from Venice, and so the glassmakers moved to Murano. At that time Venetian glass had already acquired a world-wide reputation for excellence by the high quality of the glass itself, (due perhaps to the sand from the lagoon) and the skill of the craftsmen. The glassworks were therefore one of the essential assets of the Republic. "However", wrote Guillaume Janneau in his work *"Les Arts du Feu"*, "with a thoroughly feudal lack of consistency, Venice allowed its glassmakers to suffer the most wretched poverty, even though it was their loyalty which made the city prosperous. Venice confined these craftsmen to the island of Murano and hounded, threatened or even murdered those who escaped from its tyranny".

Despite this, many of these glassworkers succeeded in reaching other countries. It was Venetians who founded the glass industry of Flanders and made it possible for that of Bohemia to reach a surpassing standard of excellence and in the 18th century supplant

that of Venice itself.

In Murano you can visit the *Glass Museum* and see the ancient glass it contains. You can also see many small glassworks where glass is blown by mouth by means of a long pipe held by the glassblower and handled, in D'Annunzio's words, with the "movements of a silent dance".

The molten glass swells, tapers and by using nothing more than the pipe is given exactly the shape intended by the craftsman. Trickles and drops are added to the main body of glass to make the most fantastic and imaginative shapes. Clever technique often supplants good taste, but nevertheless the work of these craftsmen is the central attraction of Murano.

From Burano to the Island of Solitude

Four miles from Murano is Burano, beyond doubt the most charming of all the islands in the lagoon. It is a fishing village spread over four islands. The brightly-colored housefronts are mirrored in the canals which separate the islands. Every inhabitant of Burano seems intent on preserving the charm of the place and looks after his house far better than the Venetian his palaces. The roughcast facings of the houses are freshly painted, boats are moored by the quays, fishing nets hang drying in the sun. There is always a great bustle on the quays, and here one can often see lace-makers at work with their little velvet cushions. For lace is for Burano what glass is for Murano. But the craft is carried out on a smaller scale, with stalls set up in the open air where these marvels of skill and patience done with the needle, are offered for sale to the tourists.

In the square of San Martino the campanile imitates the Leaning Tower of Pisa. Opposite it, the ancient palace of the Podesta has become a School of Lace-Making. Boats glide along the shores past washing flapping in the breeze.

The are many restaurants along the main street, and you can enjoy a fine *filet St. Pierre* washed down with a bottle of Soave, a wine from Verona, or a *fegato alla Veneziana,* which is much favored here. Gourmets will want to try the *bavolati,* snails from the lagoon.

From Burano you can take a boat to San Francesco del Deserto—also called the Island of Solitude, where St. Francis of Assisi stayed in 1220 after his return from the Holy Land. With his companion, Brother Illuminato of Rieti, Francis made a hut out of tree-branches and lived there for some time. After the Saint's death a chapel was built and finally, about 1400, the church that can be seen today. Up to the 16th century, Franciscan friars lived on the island, but then had to leave it because of the ravages of malaria. That is how it got its name of San Francesco del Deserto.

Burano: a panoramic view of its ancient houses and colorful little harbor. This is most enchanting of all the islands of the lagoon.

In later years it was setted once again by Franciscans, but in 1806 Napoleon expelled them to turn this peaceful island into a military garrison! Fifty years later the friars returned, the church was repaired and the convent extended. A few Franciscans tend the gardens round about, old cypresses watch over this island of prayer and contemplation, while on the horizon Venice floats like a mirage.

Abandoned Torcello

Artistically Torcello is the most interesting of the islands of the Lagoon. According to legend, the voice of God told the men of Altino to take refuge from the Huns on this island. They called it Turicellum (which became Torcello in Italian), because the heavenly voice had told them to climb to the top of a tower, to find this place of refuge. They settled there and founded a city which became in the course of time a warehouse for goods from Byzantium sent for sale in the Po valley. Torcello was thus a prelude to the rise of Venice which took place several centuries later.

A church was built about the beginning of the 7th century. It was enlarged in 697, when the island became an episcopal see. Traces of this church can still be seen in the lower levels of the present cathedral, which was built in the 11th century. It is in the Veneto-Byzantine style and has three naves separated by columns which are of Greek marble and surmounted by capitals. There is a mosaic floor, a 12th century iconostasis and, most notably, fine wall mosaics dating from the same period. On the wall above the entrance is a *Last Judgement,* a huge composition in five panels with a gold background. The apse has a *Virgin* showing the Madonna

Torcello: the picturesque "House of the Bishop" and the church of Santa Fosca.

wearing a blue mantle set against a gold background and accompanied by the Apostles. These mosaics of the 12th and 13th century have an advantage over those of St. Mark's in being extremely well-lit.

Near to the cathedral of Santa Maria stands the 9th century campanile and the little church of Santa Fosca built around the year 1000 in the shape of a Greek cross and surrounded by a peristyle.

These monuments are in the center of the island, where a former palace houses an archaeological museum. This delightful group of buildings can be reached from the landing stage by means of a road alongside the canal. But that is more or less all there is to see of the island of Torcello, which is nowadays uninhabited. There are meadows with, here and there, a few characterless houses. Life has withdrawn from this bygone refuge of the Venitii. Torcello is nothing more than a tourist attraction, but its mosaics alone are worth the journey.

On the Lido: a painted boat and the departure of the vaporetto. Below: typical old houses built by the fishermen of the lagoon.

The Chain of Lidi

Between the central islands and the chain of sandbanks known as *lidi,* there are islands which are rarely visited: San Erasmo and San Lazzaro degli Armeni. The latter has a monastery occupied by Armenian monks. Its library contains mementoes and a portrait of the poet Byron.

But the crowds of holidaymakers go to the Lido, the central part of the *lidi* of the lagoon. A *vaporetto* service and boats of larger tonnage provide a regular link with Venice. From the landing stage of Santa Maria Elisabette, you only have to walk a few hundred yards to the shore. There are a seaside boulevard, enclosed beaches, beach huts blocking the view and, on the other side of them, the Adriatic. It has some of the classic features of a seaside town, hotels built in an earlier period, gardens, sad villas and that nostalgia which Thomas Mann and Luchino Visconti have so skilfully conveyed in the novel and film *Death in Venice.* The beaches extend all along the coast as far as Jesolo on the mainland, where the development, set among the pine trees, is more modern.

The side of the Lido facing the lagoon is more pleasant. An avenue leads along the shore as far as the old church of San Nicolo. The sunsets over the lagoon and the horizon of Venice are often very beautiful. In the evening the lights of Venice shine and twinkle over the water.

A casino, the film center where the now defunct film festival was held and seaside villas extend as far as Alberoni. From there the coach or car you traveled in is loaded into a boat bound for the next lido, where it resumes its journey on the road to Pellestrina. The chain of sandbanks is often narrow, and the road skirting the sea has a sea-wall protecting it from the Adriatic.

The lagoon: the fishing village of Pellestrina. Right: the luxurious amenities and beaches of the Hotel Excelsior on the Lido.

Pellestrina is a fishing village with wide quays and brightly-painted houses. Here the lagoon regains its earlier aspect, that of a flat surface which is neither the surface of a lake nor that of the sea but a sort of unsilvered mirror, broken here and there by timber channel-markers and little huts built on piles where fishermen spend the night.

Pellestrina is the terminus of the bus-route and from there passenger-boats cross to Chioggia, nowadays joined to the mainland by an isthmus. It is a picturesque little town whose sole industry is fishing. It deserves a visit as much for the interesting character of its church as for the color of its canals, bridges and quays, over which hangs a smell of pickling brine.

From Venice a direct service runs to Chioggia and from there the Poldelta as far as Commacchio and Ravenna.

6. THE DESTINY OF VENICE

To understand the destiny of Venice you must understand the lagoon, its past as well as its future, for it decides the future of Venice. What fate awaits the City of the Waters at the end of this period, that of her old age? Will it be death or that transformation by which life disguises the corpses on which it feeds?

Like Rome, Venice has passed through three ages like those of mankind. From its foundation to its prime, from its birth to its maturity, it was dedicated to power and glory in all the domains of human endeavor, whether it be arms, commerce or art. From the very first centuries after the fall of Rome to the 15th century there was the brilliance which was to burst out in the 16th. And then, in the fullness of that maturity came triumph and rejoicing, followed by the beginning of that decline which was to become more and more evident until Venice was extinguished as a state.

Since the beginning of our century, Venice has been in a highly precarious situation, menaced by everything, by the times and by mankind, by science and by the elements. It is a menace which comes from the mainland, as did the earlier invaders. It is a menace which shows itself in the smoke on the northern horizon.

The lagoon while the tramontana is blowing.

Building on Sand

Venice is creation of man, not only in its monuments and its buildings but also in its site. A city built in the middle of a bay is an extreme paradox. The bay is a vast enclosed stretch of water, confined by a low-lying shore which to the north and south dwindles away into marshland. Into it pour the waters and alluvium of the alpine rivers.

These alluvial deposits carried down towards the sea are repelled by the tides, which in this stretch of the Adriatic are stronger than elsewhere in the Mediterranean. Thus were formed 120 centuries ago the chain of sandbanks known as the *lidi.* In the end they closed off the bay completely. The bay silted up, and islands were formed which appeared and disappeared with the tides. The river currents dredged deeper channels and thus preserved the water-gates through which the tides rose and fell. By this means, too, river and sea water replaced each other.

From Jesolo to Chioggia, a chain of sandbanks stretches for thirty miles. Inside this chain was created the Lagoon, henceforward protected from the sea by this natural dyke, which, however, was frail and shifting. In the Roman period, towns were founded on the shore of the mainland: Aquilea, Altinum and Fossa Clodia, which became Chioggia. In the interior lay Treviso and Padua.

Fishermen from the shore built reed huts

on the islands of the lagoon to assist them in their work, just as to this very day, near Pellestrina, they use little huts built on piles. Then came the period of foreign invasions. Here the history of Venice begins.

In the 15th century Venice was at the height of its fortunes. The conflicts which brought Venetian power to the periphery of the Adriatic and as far as the Middle East took less than a century, and the triumph of Venice coincided with the Renaissance which, first in Italy, opened up a new era. The city was filled with palaces which we still see today. The layout of Venice, its *calli, campi, campelli,* its quays and canals, all were made in accordance with local custom and in a truly exceptional communal spirit. It was the period of great artists and great commercial wealth. But in the lands beyond the sea the tide was turning against Venice. Venetian fortunes in Dalmatia and the Middle East suffered reverses, but the news made only a faint impression on Venetians minds. When the news became even worse they tried to drown it with the music of their *canzoni* and the laughter of carnival. The second age of Venice had started.

This new age was to end in disaster, though it began with the intoxication of success. However, after the beginning of the 15th century an important change had taken place. The period of hard work was succeeded by the period of enjoyment. Egle Trincanato described the situation thus: "Thus patricians of Venice have long since lost the habit which was so characteristic of them—that of conducting business themselves. Instead they have become mere administrators of riches accumulated by years of trade. This can be seen in the changed function of the Venetian palace, which formerly combined a residence with a warehouse for goods. It now became solely a noble residence."

Several decades later, Venetian life became so luxurious that a commission was formed to

inquire into "excessive pomp". It would not prevent the nobility from following the example of the Doges and the Church and keeping up appearances. Despite damage done to trade, despite the lost markets and empty coffers, the Most Serene Republic continued to live a life of luxury and enjoyment.

Auguste Bailly has this to say about those « years of madness": "Venice, though impoverished, could not forget that it had been the richest city in the world. It still had the same tastes and preferences as in its heyday. It still loved luxury, festivities, great processions of splendid state dignitaries or clergy with their banners, candles and holy relics, grand balls, jousting on the Grand Canal, masses sung beneath the gilded vault of St. Mark's, everything that was impressive and dazzling, everything which could fill life with excitement and joy."

It is difficult to imagine the sumptuousness of life in 18th century Venice. Every religious

feast-day was the pretext for celebrations. Each *sestiere* vied with others in commemorating its patron saint. Ascension Day, la *Sensa,* the Wedding of the Sea, kept up the illusion of power and importance.

Giovanni-Giacomo Casanova (1707-1793) has left us in his memoirs an impression of his period and of himself which fits the description given by Auguste Bailly in his History of Venice: "His fingers loaded with rings, his *tabarro* undone over a velvet coat adorned with gold lace, enveloped in a cloud of perfume and Spanish snuff, observing, conducting intrigues, exchanging a wink in passing with a companion of the Faro table, flirting with ladies, regaling them with moral and erotic witticisms and, more than anyone, revelling in that special atmosphere which combined lust, danger and deceit. He was by turns hired assassin, violinist, libertine, windy philosopher, thief and lawman. He would talk, with tears of sentiment in his eyes, of nature and virtue. Boaster, swindler, pedant, naively proud, frequently absurd, never subject to self-doubt, at once magnificent and disturbing, a solemn clown and unintentional buffoon who took himself seriously, in all he is the living symbol of that holiday city whose splendors were a mask for bankruptcy. Venice herself also wore a mask."

A number of painters have left impressions of Venice which are more attractive and closer to the truth: Antonio Canal, called Canaletto (1697-1768), and Francesco Guardi (1712-1795). Most of the latter's works have regrettably left Venice to find their

Such a city could not but inspire, and indeed bring forth, such great painters as Canaletto (left) and Guardi, who spent their whole lives depicting its beauty.

way to English manor-houses and galleries all over Europe. The lure of Venice, the legend fabricated by Casanova spread about in all the literary salons of Europe reached even the courts of princes. Since the beginning of the century English travelers frequented Venice and took home with them *"vedute"* to lighten the fog of their native land. From that time onwards Venice's tourist vocation became quite clear. It would help to continue the festivities to the very brink of ruin.

Every little painting by Canaletto and Guardi is a view of Venice, its festivities and riches but also its daily life and its older, seamier districts.

Above the palaces and canals they paint in vast luminous skies where the very air vibrates. They observe and depict with marvellous skill the crowded life of the quays and *campi*. They are the first painters to be the "witnesses of their times". By their qualities of delicacy, sensitivity to the poetry of the real world they are the precursors of the French landscape painters of the following century, when Corot pioneered the way for the limpid painting of the Impressionists. The absence of Canaletto and Guardi from the *Accademia* seriously distorts its representation of the major themes of Venetian painting in the 18th century.

The looseness of morals, as much as the beauty of the place, attracted all the leading personalities of Europe to Venice in the middle of the 18th century.

Goethe came in 1786. He witnessed the

93

Venetian chandeliers have long had a worldwide reputation. Below: a general view of the city seen from the campanile.

last years of the Republic. The attractiveness of the city turned to the disadvantage of the Venetian State. In Vienna the division of the remnants of Venetian territory was planned. In Junes 1796 Napoleon wrote at Verona: "I shall be the Attila of Venice!" It was not murder but robbery. The Directory ordered the removal of thirty or so pictures and more than 500 works of art and rare manuscripts. Serurier burned the "Bucintoro". The "Golden Book" was also consigned to the flames, and the horses of St. Mark were shipped to Paris.

And the festivities went on. A week after their arrival the French gave a masked ball at La Fenice, French and Venetian soldiers lining the streets. The Austrian followed the French and became even more hated than them. But Venice remained Venice. Princes stayed there, poets met there. "I had loved it since childhood" wrote Byron, "to me it was a faery city of the heart." It was precisely the place to enchant the Romantics. Chateaubriand evokes Venice in his "Mémoires d'Outre-Tombe": "The ruins of an ancient society which produced so may beautiful things gives you a distaste for a new society and leaves you without any interest in the future. You love to feel yourself dying with everything that is dying around you…"

Venice on winter days...

Saving Venice from the Waves

This nostalgia and neglect mark the third period of Venice, that of Venice now. Political events and wars have passed over her, fortunately without doing any harm. Venice has been mysteriously protected and forgotten. The scenery remains but the stage is empty.

Generations of famous people have continued to praise Venice's unique splendor. George Sand and Musset did so. Nietzsche yielded to the pleas of his friend Peter Gast:

"Here you will like everything, the air, stones, flowers, bread, *frutti di mare,* the people— an antique race, always full of life and never vulgar". Richard Wagner came to end his days here. He gave a last concert at La Fenice for his wife and a few friends, then died in the Palazzo Vendramin on 13th February 1883.

After him came Marcel Proust, Thomas Mann and and Barrès, who lamented: "Subside beneath your lagoon, Venice. The lament is heard still, but the sweet lips are dead..."